THE REACH CHALLENGE

Journal

By Joel Holm

Copyright © 2015 Joel Holm

All rights reserved.

ISBN: 0986181931
ISBN-13: 9780986181931

WELCOME TO THE CHALLENGE!

Introduction
Session 1 Ready Your Life - Pt.1
Session 2 Ready Your Life - Pt.2
Session 3 Engage Through Kindness - Pt. 1
Session 4 Engage Through Kindness - Pt. 2
Session 5 Advance to Relationship - Pt. 1
Session 6 Advance to Relationship - Pt. 2
Session 7 Connect to Community - Pt. 1
Session 8 Connect to Community - Pt. 2
Session 9 Hope in Jesus - Pt. 1
Session 10 Hope in Jesus - Pt. 2

> " Each of us should reach his neighbor for his good, to build him up."
>
> **Romans 15:2**

THEREACHCHALLENGE.COM

INTRODUCTION

Congratulations on taking the REACH Challenge. This journal is designed to help you during the next ten weeks. Each of the ten sessions is addressed in this journal. Each session gives you:

• Activities to do for each stage as part of the REACH Challenge

• Reflections to consider throughout the week to process what God is showing you

• Notes to journal your prayers and discoveries in each stage of the REACH Challenge

Activities

The REACH Challenge is an action experience. It is designed with 5 stages with action items for each stage. As you progress through each stage, the action items change to help you most effectively reach your neighbor. Each session will provide activities specifically designed for that stage. You and your team members are also encouraged to come up with your own activities.

Reflections

Each session provides three reflections for you to take a moment and consider all that God is doing in you and through you each week. Use these reflections to clarify your thoughts, fears, activities, successes, failures and whatever else you desire to write down throughout the Challenge. These reflections will help you to "take every thought captive" and be intentional in your growth through this adventure.

Notes

Take this journal with you throughout each day. You will discover that God often interrupts your daily activities with opportunity to interact with your neighbor, whether they are at work or in your neighborhood. Also be ready for those moments when God reveals a thought or experience to you. Write it down so you don't forget what you have learned.

SESSION ONE
READY YOUR LIFE
PART ONE

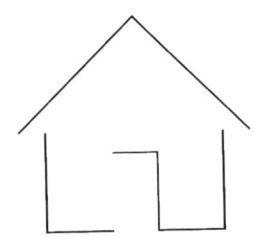

ACTIVITIES

My REACH Challenge List of Neighbors

Create a list of ten people whom you can begin to pray for throughout this REACH challenge. Some of these people may already be seeking God. Some may not want anything to do with God. Some you may know well, and others you may barely know. There are no "rules" for acquiring these ten names. Also, here are some prayer guidelines for you as you create your list of names to REACH.

Prayer guidelines for your list:

Ask God to open their spiritual eyes (2 Corinthians 4:4) .
Ask God to give them ears to hear (Matthew 13:15).
Ask God to give them faith to believe (Acts 20:21).
Ask God to give them the will to respond (Romans 10:9).
Ask God to send people into their lives to witness to them (Matthew 9:38).
Ask God for ways to build caring relationships (1 Corinthians 9:22).
Ask God for opportunities to witness (Acts 4:29).
Ask God for an opportunity to invite them to church (Luke 14:23).
Ask God to set them free from spiritual captivity (2 Timothy 2:25-26).

My REACH List:

1 _____ 2 _____

3 _____ 4 _____

5 _____ 6 _____

7 _____ 8 _____

9 _____ 10 _____

If you received a REACH bookmark, copy these names to your bookmark as well. It is important from the start of the REACH Challenge that prayer undergirds everything you do. Commit these people, and your relationship with them, to the Lord. No matter what your relationship with these ten people looks like today, through prayer and action your relationship will grow. Pray through this list of names every day. These are the individuals you will focus your faith and activity on as you complete the REACH Challenge.

REFLECTION ONE

I have become all things to all people so that by all possible means I might save some. 1 Corinthians 9:22

What does this verse mean to you personally? How is it easy for you to become all things and how is it difficult?

Take a look at your ten names and consider how you can interact with them in a way that you *become all things* to them. How can you engage your neighbors more effectively?

_____

_____

_____

_____

_____

_____

_____

_____

_____

_____

REFLECTION TWO

Though I am free from all men I made myself a servant to all that I may win more. I Corinthians 9:19

Take a moment to reflect on this thought from the Apostle Paul. What was it that enabled him to put aside his own desires and serve others? What is the connection between serving people and the REACH Challenge that will make this experience a success for you?

_____

_____

_____

_____

_____

_____

_____

_____

_____

_____

REFLECTION THREE

The god of this age has blinded the minds of unbelievers, so that they cannot see the light of the gospel that displays the glory of Christ, who is the image of God. 2 Corinthians 4:4

What does this verse teach you about what you may encounter as you begin to reach out to your neighbor? Have you experienced these *blinded minds* before and how did you handle it? You may want to raise this question with your team and see what experiences others have had and how they handled people with grace and love.

_____

_____

_____

_____

_____

_____

_____

_____

_____

_____

NOTES

SESSION TWO
READY YOUR LIFE
PART TWO

ACTIVITIES

MY TESTIMONY

Write out your testimony. It may be helpful to simply write out the main talking points of what you would present in your testimony. Some people write out the main questions they try to answer with their testimony. You don't always get a chance to share your entire testimony. Consider breaking your testimony into a few sections that could be presented individually in the right moment. No matter how you approach it, write down your testimony and spend time working on how you would share the gospel if given the opportunity.

_____

_____

_____

_____

_____

_____

_____

_____

_____

_____

REFLECTION ONE

But when he, the Spirit of truth, comes, he will guide you into all truth. He will not speak on his own; he will speak only what he hears, and he will tell you what is yet to come. John 16:13

The Holy Spirit guides us in many ways. Take time to pray for your ten names, but pay attention to the nudge of the Holy Spirit as you pray for each person. As you begin to narrow your list to the five people you will focus on during Stage Two of Engage through Kindness, be sensitive to the leading of the Holy Spirit as to who those five people should be.

_____

_____

_____

_____

_____

_____

_____

_____

_____

_____

REFLECTION TWO

And pray in the spirit on all occasions with all kinds of prayers and requests. With this in mind, be alert and always keep on praying for all the Lord's people. Ephesians 6:18

There are many ways to pray for your neighbors. You can pray for God's blessing in their lives. You can pray for their specific needs. You can worship God for creating them. If your prayers have been one type of prayer, take a few days this week and pray in a different way for them.

_____

_____

_____

_____

_____

_____

_____

_____

_____

_____

REFLECTION THREE

For our struggle is not against flesh and blood, but against the rulers, against the authorities, against the powers of this dark world and against the spiritual forces of evil in the heavenly realms. Ephesians 6:12

What does it mean that we *battle against spiritual forces*? Have you experienced this during the REACH Challenge? How can you be aware and respond to this type of spiritual battle?

_____

_____

_____

_____

_____

_____

_____

_____

_____

_____

NOTES

SESSION THREE
ENGAGE THROUGH KINDNESS
PART ONE

ACTIVITIES

INTENTIONAL KINDNESS

Welcome to the second stage of the REACH Challenge: Engage through Kindness. During the next two weeks you will do an intentional act of kindness for at least five people on your REACH Neighbor list. Below are 5 ideas for acts of kindness. Discuss more ideas with your team and make sure you link the best act of kindness to match the personality of your neighbor.

1. Food : Cook _____ and give it to _____.

2. Food : Invite _____ out to _____.

3. Service : Help _____ clean or repair their home.

4. Care : Watch _____'s children.

5. Work : Help _____ do _____ at the office.

My Team Ideas for Acts of Kindness

_____

_____

_____

_____

_____

REFLECTION ONE

And over all these virtues put on love, which binds them all together in perfect unity. Colossians 3:14

Why is love so important as part of Engaging through Kindness? Have you had a chance to show an act of kindness to your neighbor? What happened? Write down your honest reflections on the experience. What did God teach you through it?

_____

_____

_____

_____

_____

_____

_____

_____

_____

_____

REFLECTION TWO

When he saw the crowds, he had compassion on them, because they were harrassed and helpless, like sheep without a shepherd. Matthew 9:36

Take time to genuinely consider the needs of your neighbors. Think about their practical physical needs but also consider their emotional and social needs. Ask God to give you a genuine compassion for them. Consider altering your acts of kindness to better fit your neighbors' needs.

_____

_____

_____

_____

_____

_____

_____

_____

_____

_____

REFLECTION THREE

**If I give all I possess to the poor and give over my body to hardship that I may boast, but do not have love, I gain nothing.
1 Corinthians 13:3**

It is always good to continue to reflect on our motivation. After a few weeks, is the REACH Challenge losing its interest for you? Ask the Lord to instill in you a love for your neighbor that comes right from God's heart. Ask Him to give you His heart for your neighbor.

_____

_____

_____

_____

_____

_____

_____

_____

_____

_____

NOTES

SESSION FOUR
ENGAGE THROUGH KINDNESS
PART TWO

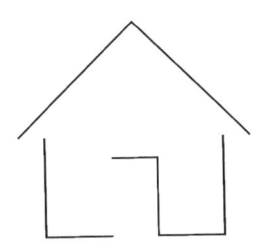

ACTIVITIES

INTENTIONAL KINDNESS

In this second week of the Engage through Kindness stage, keep doing these intentional acts of kindness. Don't worry about the size or significance of your act of kindness. God can use the smallest act for the greatest outcome. Our work is to act and pray. We leave the rest to Him. Here are a few more ideas for acts of kindness.

1. Service : Help _____ with _____ repair.

2. Service : Help _____ clean _____.

3. Care : Ask _____ for prayer requests.

4. Care : Visit _____ and listen for needs.

5. Work: Surprise _____ by doing _____ for them.

My Team Ideas for Acts of Kindness

_____

_____

_____

_____

_____

_____

REFLECTION ONE

There is no fear in love. But perfect love drives out fear, because fear has to do with punishment. The one who fears is not made perfect in love.   John 4:18

Have you experienced any fear in these first weeks of the REACH Challenge? What was it based on? Talk to your team about the fear and reflect on God's love, both for you and your neighbor, as a means of driving out that fear. What is God teaching you?

_____

_____

_____

_____

_____

_____

_____

_____

_____

_____

_____

REFLECTION TWO

Do not merely listen to the Word and so deceive yourselves. Do what it says. James 1:22

The REACH Challenge is not designed to create more stress and pressure in your life. But sometimes, in all honesty, we need a push to move us to where God wants to take us. Maybe this week is your push week. Don't fight it. Don't be overwhelmed. If it has been difficult to do the acts of kindness, reflect on why and write it out. Then write out a renewed commitment to God and ask for a clear opportunity to do an act of kindness in the next few days.

_____

_____

_____

_____

_____

_____

_____

_____

_____

REFLECTION THREE

And so we know and rely on the love God has for us. God is love. Whoever lives in love lives in God, and God in them.
1 John 4:16

Often when you love someone, you strongly sense God's love for you. Even a simple act of kindness on your part to a neighbor will amaze you at God's love for you. Have you experienced God's love for you while loving your neighbor? Describe that love and thank Him for His love. That's the love He wants you to show to your neighbor.

_____

_____

_____

_____

_____

_____

_____

_____

_____

_____

NOTES

SESSION FIVE
ADVANCE TO RELATIONSHIP
PART ONE

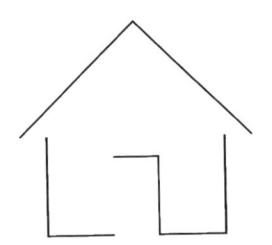

ACTIVITIES

ADVANCE TO RELATIONSHIP

Welcome to Stage Three of the REACH Challenge: Advance to Relationship. You should be proud of the past month and how God has used you to build bridges, both through prayer and action, with your neighbor for Christ. Now comes a slightly more challenging two weeks but you are good for it!

Write the names of the three people you believe should *advance to relationship*? You can write up to five if you want. The activity is not to have the right number but to have the right people. Identify those who in the past weeks have best connected to you. Pray for God's leading. Write down their names and one idea as to how you can advance the relationships.

Name : _____

Advance : _____

Name : _____

Advance : _____

Name : _____

Advance : _____

Name : _____

Advance : _____

Name : _____

Advance : _____

REFLECTION ONE

My dearest brothers and sisters, take note of this: Everyone should be quick to listen, slow to speak and slow to become angry, because human anger does not produce the righteousness that God desires. James 1:19-20

When you advance your relationship with your neighbor you run the greater risk of frustration that comes with getting to know someone. What does this verse teach you about how to advance your relationship? How can you set up a time and place where you can listen to your neighbors and show them your interest and care for their life situations?

_____

_____

_____

_____

_____

_____

_____

_____

_____

REFLECTION TWO

Opponents must be gently instructed, in the hope that God will grant them repentance leading them to a knowledge of the truth, and that they will come to their senses and escape from the trap of the devil, who has taken them captive to do his will. 2 Timothy 2:25-26

By now you have probably experienced some measure of push back from some of the neighbors you are trying to reach. How did that come about and how did it make you feel? What does this verse teach you about how to respond to that push back?

_____

_____

_____

_____

_____

_____

_____

_____

_____

REFLECTION THREE

Jesus replied: "'Love the Lord your God with all your heart and with all your soul and with all your mind.' This is the first and greatest commandment. And the second is like it: Love your neighbor as yourself." Matthew 22:37-39

Take a moment and hit the pause button in this REACH Challenge. Reflect once again on God's love for you. Have you found yourself so busy with life and even with the Challenge that you haven't made time to experience His love, through prayer, worship and His Word? Take this time to *abide* in Jesus. Let Him rekindle His love. Write out your thanks to Him and express your love to Him.

_____

_____

_____

_____

_____

_____

_____

_____

NOTES

SESSION SIX
ADVANCE TO RELATIONSHIP
PART TWO

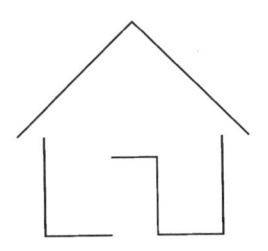

ACTIVITIES

CONTINUING THE ADVANCE

Relationships take time. The REACH Challenge time frame won't give you enough time to fully develop a relationship with your neighbor. That's not the goal. This stage takes you from an acquaintance to a friend. Being a friend to your unreached neighbor may be a much longer pursuit. So the goal of this stage is simply to get the friendship going.

For that reason this week's activity is a second round of advance ideas for you with your three neighbors. Write the names of the three people you are working to advance to a relationship. Again, you can write up to five if you want. If you've had some interaction with them, write out a possible next step for building the friendship. If you've not been able to yet, then write again your first step in getting to know them better.

ADVANCE TO RELATIONSHIP

Name : _____

Advance : _____

Name : _____

Advance : _____

Name : _____

Advance : _____

Name : _____

Advance : _____

Name : _____

Advance : _____

REFLECTION ONE

Love is patient, love is kind. It does not envy, it does not boast, it is not proud. 1 Corinthians 13:4

Describe your activities for advancing to relationship. What were the struggles? What advancement took place in your relationship with your neighbor? How can you see God at work?

_____

_____

_____

_____

_____

_____

_____

_____

_____

_____

_____

_____

REFLECTION TWO

**Love does not dishonor others, it is not self seeking, it is not easily angered, it keeps no record of wrongs.
1 Corinthians 13:5**

Write out the four traits of love described in this verse. How do these characteristics of love affect how you do the REACH Challenge? What do they teach you about how to *love your neighbor*? When might you be tempted not to live out these traits of love with your neighbor?

_____

_____

_____

_____

_____

_____

_____

_____

_____

_____

REFLECTION THREE

Love does not delight in evil but rejoices with the truth. It always protects, always trusts, always hopes, always perseveres. I Corinthians 13 6-7

The REACH Challenge is not designed to be done alone. Reflect on your team and those who are providing support to you. What are they teaching you about God's love by how they are protecting, trusting, hoping and persevering with you?

_____

_____

_____

_____

_____

_____

_____

_____

_____

_____

NOTES

SESSION SEVEN
CONNECT TO COMMUNITY
PART ONE

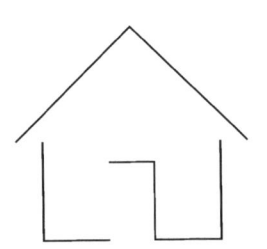

ACTIVITIES

CONNECT TO COMMUNITY

You have moved from Ready Your Life to Engage through Kindness to Advance to Relationship and now you are ready for Stage Four of the REACH Challenge: Connect to Community. This is the stage you have been waiting for because you now get to invite others to be part of reaching your neighbor. Jesus always sent people out in teams. This is the heart of Connect to Community.

Your activity is to write the names of your neighbors down and then select one of three ways presented on the video for connecting your neighbor to your Christ- centered community. You can connect them to your church. You can connect them to a small group. (This doesn't have to be formal small group but any smaller grouping of believers.) And you can connect them to a community outreach that exposes them to serving alongside Christians.

Connect to Community

(check one box and write out action plan)

My Neighbor: _____
☐ Invite to Church   ☐ Invite to Smaller Group   ☐ Invite to Community Outreach
Action Plan:_____

My Neighbor: _____
☐ Invite to Church   ☐ Invite to Smaller Group   ☐ Invite to Community Outreach
Action Plan:_____

My Neighbor: _____
☐ Invite to Church   ☐ Invite to Smaller Group   ☐ Invite to Community Outreach
Action Plan:_____

My Neighbor: _____
☐ Invite to Church   ☐ Invite to Smaller Group   ☐ Invite to Community Outreach
Action Plan:_____

My Neighbor: _____
☐ Invite to Church   ☐ Invite to Smaller Group   ☐ Invite to Community Outreach
Action Plan:_____

REFLECTION ONE

And pray for us, too, that God may open a door for our message, so that we may proclaim the mystery of Christ, for which I am in chains. Colossians 4:3

Paul asked for prayer for *open doors*. This is a good prayer request for you as well. Take this time to pray for the other members of your team. Pray that they would have open doors. Write their names out and write out your *open door* prayer for them.

_____

_____

_____

_____

_____

_____

_____

_____

_____

_____

_____

REFLECTION TWO

And let us consider how we may spur one another on toward love and good deeds. Hebrew 10:24

When you Connect to Community, you are intentionally involving your neighbor in your Christ-centered family relationships. As others are helping you reach your neighbor, consider who you can help in reaching their neighbor? Who can you encourage towards love and good deeds?

_____

_____

_____

_____

_____

_____

_____

_____

_____

_____

REFLECTION THREE

If you declare with your mouth, "Jesus is Lord", and believe in your heart that God raised him from the dead, you will be saved. Romans 10:9

God may give you an opportunity to present the gospel to your neighbor. Pray for these opportunities. Remember your neighbor is not joining a church or reciting a creed. What does it mean to *believe in your heart* and to *confess with your mouth*? How can you lead your neighbor to do these two things?

_____

_____

_____

_____

_____

_____

_____

_____

_____

_____

NOTES

SESSION EIGHT
CONNECT TO COMMUNITY
PART TWO

ACTIVITIES

CONNECT TO COMMUNITY

Along with connecting your neighbors to your church, your small group or simply your Christian friends, how can you and your family connect better to your community? How can you add value to your community? Make a list of ways that you can serve your community, from specific prayer walk times to volunteering in your community. If you have children, consider how you can include them in these activities.

_____

_____

_____

_____

_____

_____

_____

_____

_____

_____

_____

REFLECTION ONE

Be wise in the way you act toward outsiders; make the most of every opportunity. Let your conversation be always full of grace, seasoned with salt, so that you may know how to answer everyone. Colossians 4:5-6

Life is full of opportunities. Do you find your days get so busy that you sense you are missing opportunities God sets in front of you? Try to recall opportunities this past week where you could have reached out to a neighbor but you didn't. Don't be too hard on yourself. Learn from it and grow. How can you slow your life down so as not to miss God's opportunities?

_____

_____

_____

_____

_____

_____

_____

_____

_____

REFLECTION TWO

For God so loved the world that he gave his one and only Son, that whoever believes in him shall not perish but have eternal life. John 3:16

You have probably read this verse many times over. Try to read it with a fresh look. What does it tell you about God and about your neighbors? What does it teach you about how you should live in your community? Draw out some new insights and prayerfully reflect on them.

_____

_____

_____

_____

_____

_____

_____

_____

_____

_____

_____

REFLECTION THREE

**For all have sinned and fall short of the glory of God.
Romans 3:23**

How does this simple truth affect your relationships? Why is it so important to remember this truth when reaching out to your neighbors? What can happen when you forget this? Write out your thoughts and write a prayer in response to this verse.

_____

_____

_____

_____

_____

_____

_____

_____

_____

_____

_____

NOTES

SESSION NINE
HOPE IN JESUS
PART ONE

ACTIVITIES

HOPE IN JESUS

You made it. Well almost! This last stage, Hope In Jesus, is as important (if not more so) than any other stage. You've worked hard these past weeks to reach your neighbor with the love of Christ. But perhaps you haven't *sealed the deal* with them. Maybe it didn't go as easy and fast as you thought. It's critical that during this last stage you work just as hard in turning your neighbor over to Jesus. Your neighbor belongs to Him.

Write out your neighbors' names and next to them, write a prayer to the Lord, giving those neighbors to Him. Include how you will continue to serve the Lord by engaging with your neighbor. Ask the Lord to protect you from any feelings of guilt or failure.

Name : _____
Prayer : _____

Name : _____
Prayer : _____

Name : _____
Prayer : _____

Name : _____
Prayer : _____

Name : _____
Prayer : _____

REFLECTION ONE

Give thanks to the Lord for He is good. His love endures forever. Psalms 136:1

Reflect on how God has been good to you during the REACH Challenge. How has He shown Himself to you? What did He do in you and through you that you were not expecting?

_____

_____

_____

_____

_____

_____

_____

_____

_____

_____

_____

REFLECTION TWO

For the wages of sin is death, but the gift of God is eternal life in Christ Jesus our Lord. Romans 6:23

Go back to your original list of ten names from week one. Pray for each of them. Pray that they would receive this *gift* from God. Ask God to continue to grow in you, far after the REACH Challenge is done, a passion to pray for the salvation of your neighbors.

REFLECTION THREE

But God demonstrates his own love for us in this: While we were still sinners, Christ died for us. Romans 5:8

Throughout the REACH Challenge you may have been reminded how you used to be before coming to Christ. What has God revealed to you through the REACH Challenge about His grace, both for you and for your neighbor?

_____

_____

_____

_____

_____

_____

_____

_____

_____

_____

_____

NOTES

SESSION TEN
HOPE IN JESUS
PART TWO

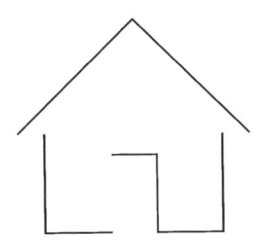

ACTIVITIES

CELEBRATE IN JESUS!

Take this week to reflect on the lessons you learned through the REACH Challenge. Use the questions below to help you reflect and verbalize how you have grown.

- How has your faith grown?
- How has your awareness of your neighbors changed?
- How has your identity in Christ developed?
- What's different about you?
- What fears have you overcome?
- What new aspect of God have you discovered?
- What did you learn about the world through this challenge?
- Why did God want you to take on the REACH Challenge?

REFLECTION ONE

Read the Lord's Prayer in Matthew 6:9-13. Use the video teaching as a guide to pray for your neighbors.

REFLECTION TWO

His Master replied, "Well done good and faithful servant! You have been faithful with a few things; I will put you in charge of many things. Come and share your Master's happiness."
Matthew 25:21

It's a good exercise to reflect on how your work through the REACH Challenge blessed your Father in Heaven. List some ways you blessed Him. Be humble and grateful for the opportunity to serve Him. Celebrate with Him all that He did through you.

_____

_____

_____

_____

_____

_____

_____

_____

_____

REFLECTION THREE

Each of us should REACH his neighbor for his good, to build him up. Romans 15:2

You started ten weeks ago with this verse at the front of this journal. Finish the REACH Challenge by writing a prayer of thanksgiving to God for how He has transformed you through this challenge.

_____

_____

_____

_____

_____

_____

_____

_____

_____

_____

_____

_____

NOTES

Made in the USA
Charleston, SC
19 June 2016